C000070322

THE CTS COMPANION
TO THE ANGELS

by
J.B. Midgley

*All booklets are published thanks to the
generous support of the members of the
Catholic Truth Society*

CATHOLIC TRUTH SOCIETY
PUBLISHERS TO THE HOLY SEE

---✠---

"We believe in One God, Son and Holy Spirit,

Creator of things visible,

such as the world in which our brief life

runs its course, and of things invisible,

such as the pure spirits which are called angels.

(Profession of Faith, Pope Paul VI, 1968)

---✠---

Angel sent by God to guide me,

Be my light and walk beside me;

Be my guardian and protect me;

On the paths of life direct me.

(Prayer to our Guardian Angel)

CONTENTS

INTRODUCTION

This booklet invites us to consider again the Angels -
those who share our dwelling in time and space and whose
existence is entwined with our own. It would be a pity if
Angels were remembered only when Christmas carols
were sung, cards written or shining examples fixed to the
tops of conifer trees. In acknowledging the angels, we
join in their adoration of our Creator and thank Him for
their creation and ours. Awareness of the guardian angels
is a special comfort for which to be grateful. This
companion considers the nature and activity of angels,
how some, led by Satan, disobeyed God and the effects
this fall from grace had upon our own history of salvation.
The inspiration is the Church's belief and teaching, her
protection against misunderstandings about the world of
the spirit, and her Feasts and Liturgy by which she guides
devotion to illuminate doctrine and support the prayerful
habits of Faith which keep it vibrant.

*(J.B. Midgley, Downham Market, Feast of the Guardian
Angels, 1999).*

THE ANGELS

What the Church Believes

In 1215, the Lateran Council made a statement of belief which formed the basis of a more specific definition by the Vatican Council of 1870. "God created spiritual beings we call angels and our own visible, material world out of nothing by His almighty power. Afterwards, again from nothing, He made a creature of both body and soul we call man, an act of His goodness because, being infinite, His happiness needed no addition. He wished only to reveal His perfections by the blessings He bestows on His creatures. The angels are the friends and companions of our spiritual life and their closeness to God helps to deepen our relationship with Him."

In 1950, Pope Pius XII reminded the faithful that, in their intelligence and will, the angels surpass the visible creation; that they glorify God without ceasing and, as His messengers, co-operate in His plan of salvation; that their obedience, zeal and love of God are examples for our imitation; and that, because they are so happily placed, we can call on them with total confidence. It will be noticed that, when she recites the Litany of the Saints, the Church asks for the help of St Michael and all the Holy Angels immediately after the Most Blessed Virgin and before all others.

Angels in the Bible

In the Divine Revelation of Holy Scripture, we have God's own word that, throughout our lives, the angels watch over us carefully and intercede for us. The Book of Job says that there is an angel always at our side, ready to remind us where our duty lies and Psalm 34, that one pitches camp around those who fear God and keeps them safe. Of their protective role more will be said in the final chapter, 'The Principle Feasts'.

In St Luke's Gospel *(16:21)*, we read of the death of Lazarus, the beggar, and how the angels carry his soul to Abraham's bosom, an intimation of our own arrival in "a heavenly Jerusalem where millions of angels are gathered with the whole Church for the festival where everyone is a first born citizen." *(Heb 12:21-24)*.

God's word is sensitive to our problems in understanding what we do not see and concentrates more on what angels do than what they are. For example, they close Paradise after the banishment of Adam and Eve, "cherubs and the flame of a flashing sword guarding the way to the Tree of Life." *(Gn 3:24)*. They protect Lot, his wife and two daughters from the destruction which overtakes Sodom *(Gn 19:5-16)* and God employs them to announce the birth of children and forecast their destinies. To Hagar, the slave-girl of Abraham and Sarah, an angel says, "Go back to your mistress and submit to her... Now you have conceived and you will bear a son and you shall name him Ishmael... A wild ass of a man he shall be, against every man and every man against him..." *(Gn 16:11-12)*. Another tells Abraham he will visit him again next year when Sarah herself will give birth to Isaac who will be one of the early Patriarchs. *(Gn 18:9-15)*. Then, an "angel of God" visits the wife of Manoah and says, "You are barren and have no child but... you will conceive and bear a son... It is he who will begin to rescue Israel from the power of the Philistines" and he will be called Samson. *(Jg 13:6-8)*.

The wonderful coherence of the Divine Plan is preparing us for the news to Elizabeth concerning John the Baptist, Christ's herald, and Gabriel's incomparable Annunciation to Mary. There are other instances of angelic involvement. When Israel's army is beleaguered by its enemy, an angel, having marched at its vanguard, then brings a pillar of cloud to its rear so that it is hidden from attack, *(Ex 14:19)*, and another saves Jerusalem from Syrian invaders. Again, it is an angel who stays Abraham's hand when he is about to sacrifice his son Isaac. God has tested Abraham's fidelity but, with the messenger's intervention, He shows us that He will not hesitate to sacrifice His own beloved Son for the sake of mankind. *(Gn 22:11-12)*.

Angels and the Prophets

The Prophets did not have the most enviable of tasks. Very often, when they were required to bring distasteful news to God's people, they betrayed an understandable reluctance or a sense of unworthiness if called to announce the plan of salvation. Some were even irritated when , having threatened fire and brimstone on erring mortals, they were covered with embarrassment when unexpected repentance averted the promised disaster. However, angels would fly to sustain and encourage them. When Isaiah felt overwhelmed by the responsibility of foretelling the momentous news of the Incarnation, "One of the seraphs flew to (him), holding in his hand a live coal which he had taken from the altar... With this he touched (his) lips and said...' your sin is taken away; your iniquity is purged.'" *(Is 6:6-8).*

Visits by Angels

The image of the angels and our view of their activities owe a great deal to Scriptural representation of the Court of Heaven where Almighty God is surrounded by ministers who carry out His wishes. The prophet Micah told Ahab, the King of Israel, that he had seen the Lord, seated on His throne, and the hosts of Heaven "arrayed at His right hand and at His left." *(1 K 22:19-23).* Isaiah saw God seated on a high throne, His train filling the sanctuary and the seraphs singing the hymn of praise in which, even today, we join our voices in the Eucharist. "Holy, Holy, Holy is the Lord of Hosts. His glory fills the whole earth." *(6:1-7)*.

Artistic convention gives the angels wings but, as often as not, when they come to the aid of their earthly companions they adopt a human appearance. When Abraham was sitting outside his tent at the Oak of Mamre in the heat of the day and, no doubt, pondering on what he next should do. it was "three men" who came to visit him. *(Gn 18:1-2)*. Perhaps it was because, after their return from exile, the people of God held Him in such awe that He seemed remote from human affairs. In His kindness, He allowed His angels to arrive as humans so that they would be the less astonishing and, therefore, the more effective intermediaries.

Angels as Sons of God

In the Old Testament, both the angels and men are accorded the title 'Sons of God' which underlines a shared, adoptive sonship and the intimacy of relationship God the Father extends to all His creatures. "You are the sons of God," says Deuteronomy *(14:1)*, "a people chosen to be His very own." The prophet Hosea not only reveals more of God's tenderness but also gives a proleptic hint about the Son of God's return from exile with Mary and Joseph and the kinship we enjoy with Jesus Christ: "When Israel was a child I loved him and I called my son out of Egypt. Job *(38:4-7)* is given a glorious vision of all the angels, "the stars of the morning, singing with joy, the sons of God chanting praise" as the Creator lays the foundations of the material world. They rejoice for us because they know that the harmony of creation is what God wills and we, like them, are stars of the morning and sons of God present in His mind from all eternity as co-heirs with His beloved Son.

Angels in the New Testament

God's single plan of salvation, is revealed in the coherence of the Old and New Testaments. So we find the instances of angelic help and companionship in the 'Acts of the Apostles'. The High Priest and the Saducees were so enraged by the Apostles' enviable success, that they put aside their differences to engineer their imprisonment but the angel of the Lord liberated them by opening the gates. He told them to go to the Temple itself and give the people the news of the new life in Christ. They found the courage to do this, not behind closed doors, but in a most sacred and public place.

Another angel advises the Apostle Philip, about to travel from Jerusalem to Gaza, to take the desert road. This was not a route likely to appeal to a missioner zealous to find listeners for his preaching. Nevertheless, he follows the angel's advice and, as a result, meets the Ethiopian, a member of a race held in low esteem, and converts him to the Faith. Through the angel, God has conveyed the message that He knows which ways are best and that following them brings the happiest results. *(Ac 5:18-21; 8:26-32).*

By now, it may have crossed some minds that there is quite enough to do in concentrating upon the essential truth of God's existence without having to cope with unseen hosts of angels who live in an equally invisible world. After all, we know that, in the workings of Divine Providence, the mediation of Christ is all sufficient and needs no addition and, furthermore, we enjoy the omnipotent protection of a Father who loves us with boundless intensity. Why then, do we contemplate this mission of the angels and their involvement in our destiny? As always, we look for our answer to Him "through whom all things came to be." *(Jn 1:3).*

The angels and Jesus Christ

St Paul glimpses the splendour of the Son of God, the true likeness of the God we do not see and who is the source of all creation. "In Him were created all things in Heaven and earth, visible and invisible, Thrones, Dominations, Sovereignties, Powers, all things were created through Him and for Him." *(1 Col 1:15-16).*

These lines are part of a Christological hymn which celebrates the harmony of creation. Our world is linked to another, different but equally wonderful and diverse, and every creature, from the lowest to those closest to God's throne, has steps on the ladder which was shown to Jacob in his dream. "It was standing on the ground with the top reaching to Heaven; and there were angels of God going up it and coming down. And the Lord was there, standing over him saying, 'I am the Lord, the God of Abraham your father, and the God of Isaac." *(Gn 28:12-13)*.

The orders of angels mentioned by St Paul are part of the teaching of the Church which Christians accept and to which they subscribe by an act of faith. The Nicene Creed, for example, is proclaimed during the Mass, the central act of worship, at a significant moment between the Gospel Reading and the Eucharistic Liturgy. "We believe in One God, the Father Almighty, Maker of heaven and earth, of all that is seen and unseen." Christ has explained that, from the 'beginning' the creation of the angels and of men came together in the mind of the Word through whom all things were made and that they share the same end, happiness in the glory of the beatific Vision. "Those who are judged worthy of a place in the other world and in the resurrection of the dead are as the angels and, being children of the Resurrection, are sons of God." *(Lk 20:35-36)*.

During His earthly life when He shares our material existence, Jesus Christ is adored and worshipped by the angels from the moment of His Incarnation until His Ascension. He does, indeed, make "His angels winds and His servants flames of fire." *(Heb 1:5-8)*. They bring to

His Mother, Mary, the most momentous news in all
creation when Gabriel announces His conception. Angels
proclaim His Birth and protect Him during His vulnerable
infancy by guiding Joseph, His foster-father, to take the
family to Egypt and then, later, back to Nazareth. They
come to take care of Him when, after His forty days' fast
in the desert in preparation for His act of Redemption, He
has put Satan to flight. One comforts Him during His
agony in the Garden on the night before He gives His life
to free human nature from the slavery of sin, and another
announces the triumph of His Resurrection. When, at His
Ascension, He has left our sight, "two men in white"
comfort us in the person of the Apostles. "Jesus, who has
been taken up from you into Heaven...will come back in
the same way as you have seen Him go." *(Ac 1:10-11)*.
At last, when He will come again in glory on the clouds
of Heaven, the angels will accompany Him to serve His
judgment *(cf Mt 24:30-31)* and "The voice of the
Archangel will call the command and the Lord Himself
will come down from Heaven. Those who have died in
Christ will be the first to rise... So we shall stay with the
Lord forever." *(1 Th 4:13-18)*.

Christ speaks to us about His angels

Our Lord leaves us in no doubt that the angels have a part
to play in the realisation of God's plan. Whenever He
speaks of them, He does so with an emphatic solemnity

which asks for our close attention. "I tell you, there is rejoicing among the angels of God over one repentant sinner." *(Lk 15:10)*. "I tell you, if anyone openly declares himself for me in the presence of men, the Son of Man will openly declare Himself for him in the presence of God's angels." *(Lk 9:26)*. "See that you never despise one of these little children for, I tell you, their angels in Heaven are continually in the presence of my Father." *(Mt 18:10)*.

What He says about an immense spiritual world is in the context of our lives in the material world during which we prepare to join His angels. Little children, for example, may not invariably behave like angels but their innocence and trusting dependence, their willingness to make confident leaps of faith teach an awareness beyond the mundane.

As the time of His suffering and death approaches, the Lord of all creation tells an ever-protective Peter to put away his sword because He had only to ask His Father and twelve legions of angels would be sent to defend Him. The seed he has sown will come to fruition in His Church and it is His angels who will assist Him when He gathers the harvest *(cf Mt 13:41-42)* and who will be His witnesses when He welcomes us to His side *(cf Lk 9:26)*.

What Christ says helps us to an easier, more assured, acceptance that the co-existence of angels and men is His will and that the spiritual and material spheres are harmonised in Him. In a brighter light we believe in the Communion of Saints, the marvellous assembly, in His Body, of His pilgrims on earth, the faithful departed,the angels and saints, all united in an exchange of prayer, intercession, merits and in the adoration of their Creator whose intentions are eternally fulfilled.

THE CELESTIAL HIERARCHY

Although Christ, the King of Angels and of Men, did not go into great descriptive detail about the angelic world, the serious tone with which He spoke of the angels aroused particular interest among His earliest followers. Naturally, they already knew about the angel both from the Old Testament and their oral tradition, but now they began to take a closer look at the aura and influence of their angelic companions. The product of any consequent, speculative theology is not to be confused with the guarantees of teaching which is based on Divine Revelation and the apportioning of ranks, duties and activities is not a matter of faith. It is, however, a deduction from Scripture and tradition which stems from devotion and worth considering in that it presents, in human terms, a sharper image of the spiritual world.

Early writings about angels

The Judaic, 'apocalyptic' writings, so called after the final book of the New Testament, were known and revered by the early Christians. Mindful of Jacob's ladder, they began to identify an order which illustrated degrees of perfection between the material world and God. The early Fathers, like St Jerome and his fourth century contemporary St Ambrose, gave much thought to the organization of a Celestial Hierarchy and their work was developed by St Gregory the Great in the sixth century and St John Damascene in the eighth. The detailed arrangement which seems to have exercised the widest influence, however, is the work of Denys, or Dionysius, the Areopagite who had adopted the name of St Paul's distinguished convert mentioned in the 'Acts of the Apostles' *(17:34)*.

Denys had been much influenced by the theology and mysticism of Evagrios of Pontos who had been an eminent member of the Council of Constantinople in 381 before his death around 400 AD. His list of nine choirs of angels in three hierarchical divisions owes something to Evagrios and, in its turn, was to intrigue mediaeval scholastics like St Thomas Aquinas *(1225-74)* who used the classification in his reflections on the material and spiritual spheres and for his teaching on the Eucharist and transubstantiation.

Apart from the 'Celestial Hierarchy', Denys' best known works are 'The Mystical Theology' and 'The Divine Names'. He sought to bring together the patristic traditions of mystical theology because he felt that, as believers, we are all 'mystics' since we are immersed in the mystery of Christ through Baptism, the Scriptures and the Liturgy and our souls progress from signs and concepts to be transformed in the mystery of Divine Love. He also emphasised the importance of 'positive' theology, that which can be affirmed about God as He reveals Himself in Creation, Scripture and Liturgy and found the mystical and the positive to be interdependent. He died about 500 AD.

Seraphim, Cherubim, Thrones

The prophet Isaiah, to whom artistic convention acknowledges a debt, describes the Seraphim as having six wings, two to cover the face because God is so radiantly glorious, two at their feet and two with which to fly. Their name means "burning ones", describing their ardent devotion when they participate in Heaven's liturgy as they sing God's praises around His throne. *(6:2-7)*.

The Cherubim are of similar status in their attendance upon God and it was they who stood guard over Eden to bar entry after the fall of Adam and Eve. When Solomon, the King of Israel, was about to build his Great Temple in Jerusalem, he remembered that God had directed Moses to make a throne of mercy with the figures of two golden cherubs at either end. *(Ex 26:18-21)*. And so it was that their representation came to be included.

Thrones, as we know, are mentioned by St Paul as part of God's creation in Christ. He would have been familiar Judaic tradition's identification of seventy such angels and that some of them were among those believed to have joined with Satan. The faithful ones are known for their steadfastness and Denys thought that God selects them to demonstrate His justice when the occasion arises.

Dominations, Virtues, Powers

Dominations, as one might guess, are in charge of other angels as they carry out their various tasks which show forth the majesty of the Creator. As emblems of their authority they have the orb and sceptre which, to our own day, remain the symbols of benevolent power. Virtues, in the Hebrew tradition, are those appointed by God to work His miracles when they are appropriate to His Providence but they have other responsibilities as well. The "two men in white robes", for instance, who stood with the Apostles as Christ ascended in Heaven, are reputed to be Virtues.

Powers have been the subject of differing opinions. St Paul thinks that they, with the Sovereignties, were adherents of Satan and that, together, they make up the "spiritual army of evil in the heavens who originate the darkness in this world," *(Ep 6:12-13)* and he numbers them among those who cannot "separate us from the love of God in Christ Jesus Our Lord." *(Rm 8:38-39)*. Denys sees them in a kinder light and explains that they thwart the efforts of those demons who hate man and try to overthrow the world. St Gregory, likewise, understands them to have a restraining influence on those angels who turned away from God.

Principalities, Archangels, Angels

Principalities are entrusted with the protection of Religion, the guardianship of the Churches and the support of the people's leaders to whom they suggest wise choices. With Powers and Sovereignties, St Paul includes them in the ranks of evil as well as good spirits.

Archangels are God's chief messengers who carry out His decrees. The apocryphal First Book of Enoch, commemorating a son of Cain and the father of Methuselah, reveals an interest in the mystical, speculative and cosmic characteristics of Jewish thought and names seven: Uriel, Raguel, Michael, Seraquel, Gabriel, Hamil and Raphael. Michael, Gabriel and Raphael are well known to us through Holy Scripture will be considered more fully in the context of their Feast.

Angels do not seem to have acquired individual names despite their frequent appearances as helpful humans in the Old Testament. In fact, when Manoah, who was to be the father of Samuel, asked the angel his name so that he could be honoured when his promise was fulfilled, God's messenger preferred to remain anonymous. "Why ask me my name?" he replied. "It is a mystery." *(Jg 13:17).* What is important is that the angels execution of judgment guidance, protection, healing and intercession reveal how, for our well-being, God employs them in our salvation and so draws us to Himself.

THE FALL OF THE ANGELS

The human intellect and vocabulary find themselves at something of a loss when confronted with what appears to be an act of folly on a grand scale. Pure spirits of sublime intelligence and will, made a conscious decision to throw away every advantage and distort the reason for their existence. The event is perplexing but we can draw from it certain lessons and conclusions about ourselves and our own downfall from which it cannot be disassociated.

Freedom to choose

Angels and men are the creative outcome of God's infinite goodness and love. Though His love desires reciprocation, His goodness does not demand or compel and He has given His creatures the dignity of freedom and personality. Because He is all goodness, only goodness can proceed from Him and all the angels were created good. They were capable of loving obedience to the One on whom their existence depended and who knows best. Once the opportunity had been taken to demonstrate such loving obedience they were destined to enjoy the full vision of God, their Creator, for all eternity. It was not so much that God wanted to try them out as the reality that there can be no happiness without love. Love, however, is not to be constrained, is offered freely but freedom is meaningless unless there is a choice.

If they were true to their nature and fulfil their existence, the angels would choose to love God through obedience and service, would choose Him and what He offered before their own limitations. Pure spirits are immortal and do not dwell in time so we do not know what period elapsed between their creation and the opportunity either to give God His due by an act of free will or to reject their destiny. Of all the angels, none was more beautiful, intelligent and powerful which is why he is sometimes called Lucifer, the "carrier of light", once the brightest "star of the morning". Because of the gifts he had received, he was also the more 'willful', the more capable of exercising choice with irreversible deliberation. He and those of like mind were seduced by self-love and pride to imagine to reign in their own world we now call hell than serve in Heaven. They forgot their dependence in their hurry to be their own gods, so they opted for hatred instead of love, enmity instead of friendship and darkness instead of glory.

A Battle in Heaven

Within each pure spirit, created individually, a personal battle took place. It was not possible for an angel to sin through bodily senses such as man possesses. Sin could be committed only in the intellect. Satan and his followers, though not divine, decided to be gods themselves and such rebellious pride motivated a choice which, once made, was not to be withdrawn. Scripture does not tell us how long it took the angels to determine whether to love God or turn to disobedience, only that there was a fierce battle in Heaven fought between Satan, with his rebel forces, and the faithful angels led by Michael. "And now war broke out in heaven, when Michael with his angels attacked the dragon. The dragon fought back with his angels but they were defeated and driven out of heaven. The great dragon, the primeval serpent, known as the devil or Satan, who had deceived the world, was hurled down to the earth and his angels were hurled down with him. His tail dragged a third of the stars from the sky and dropped them to the earth." *(Rv 12:7-12;4)*.

No forgiveness wanted

Having denied their nature through such a mistake, why did these extraordinarily intelligent beings not have feelings of regret? Why were these erstwhile stars of the morning, and so dear to God, not given the grace of repentance? The answer lies in the very superiority of their being which, St Augustine and others concluded, gave their sin a deadly finality. God's infinite mercy and forgiveness is never to be doubted but the rebels wanted neither.

Forgiveness has to be accepted as well as given before it is complete. The angelic spirit, before it reaches any conclusion, intuitively and instantly comprehends every positive and negative circumstance of the choice to be freely made so that, once the choice is made, there is no re-consideration and no alternative is even contemplated. The inspired intelligence accepts that sin which is not followed by repentance remains unforgiven, not because God withholds mercy but because it is not wanted. The position is similar to that which we, here on earth, call the sin of "final impenitence". When the immortal soul has left the human body at death, it is fixed in its state and is now subject to the same laws which apply to pure spirits. Just as the souls of the just and the faithful angels do not withdraw their love for God, so the souls of the impenitent and the fallen angels do not withdraw their hatred.

Satan: No ordinary angel

The pure spirit exists not in that which we call "time", but in an "eternal present". When Satan was reaching a decision, he was able to comprehend the privileges which would be accorded to some new race of human beings. He knew that the Word of God, his own Maker, would take the nature of man by actually joining this inferior, but inexplicably favoured species. He saw that Christ, in the one Person of God the Son, would unite human nature with His own divine nature in which no angel would ever have a share, "for the One who sanctified and the ones who are sanctified are of the same stock." (*Heb 2:10-11*).

For Satan worse was to come. When Jesus Christ had redeemed mankind by His death and Resurrection, He

would take His human nature and glorified body back to
the coveted Godhead and then share His Kingdom with
His human brothers and sisters who would fill the places
in Heaven vacated by the "third of the stars" whose pride
would take them to perdition. Mary, the Woman who as
Mother of Christ would be the agent of His Incarnation
and victory, would be taken, with her body, from the
material to the spiritual world to be crowned Queen of
Heaven and the Angels for all eternity.

This was all too much for Satan and confirmed his "I
will not serve". Even if doomed to failure, he would
oppose God's plan and at least make an attempt to ruin
mankind. He would misuse his superior intelligence and
powers to persuade these people to choose themselves
before God and reject the moral order by disobeying
Him. "It was envy that brought death into the world, as
those who are the devil's partners will discover." *(Ws
2:24)*.

Our First Parents

"Those whom the Lord begot unblemished have become
crooked, false, perverse. Is it thus you repay the Lord,
senseless and foolish people? Is it not your Father who
created you, He who made you, on whom you depend?"
(Dt 32:12).

When the devil first tempted Eve by beckoning her
down the path he himself had followed, he sounded totally

convincing. "Did God really say you were not to eat from any of the trees in the Garden? Surely not! You won't die. He knows that when you eat the fruit, your eyes will open and you will be gods like him, able to distinguish good from evil." *(cf. Gn 3:1-5)*. As with the angels, man was given a chance to show love for his Creator by exercising a free choice to obey but the opportunity was missed. Adam, after Eve, ate of the fruit and the human race, hitherto unconscious of evil, was inveigled to suspend trust in its Creator and abuse freedom by the disobedience which was to characterise all subsequent sin. Eyes were indeed opened, but at such a cost.

The Victory of Jesus Christ

"Then I saw an Angel coming down from Heaven with the key of the abyss in his hand and an enormous chain. He overpowered the dragon, that primeval serpent which is the devil and Satan." *(Rv 20:2-10)*. "It was to undo all that the devil had done that the Son of God appeared." *(1 Jn 3:8)*. In the New Covenant, the devil tried to divert the Son of God from the saving mission which had been entrusted to Him by His Father. Christ, at the end of His fast in the desert *(Mt 4:1-11)*, allows Satan to tempt Him in three ways: to give way to sensuality, to seek temporal wealth and power and to put God to the test. Where the first Adam failed, the Second chooses obedience to His Father's will and His victory foreshadows the eternal triumph of the Redemption. "As one man's fall brought condemnation on everyone, so the good act of one man brings everyone life and makes them justified. As by one man's disobedience many were made sinners, so by one man's obedience many will be made righteous." *(Rm 5:17-19)*.

Although he had exhausted his supply of temptations, Satan was later to return "at the appointed time" when he was again to persecute Christ and bring Him to His suffering. *(cf Lk 4:13)*. "This is the reign of darkness", says the Saviour *(Luke 22:53)* and adds "I shall not walk with you any longer because the prince of this world is on his way." *(Jn 14:30)*. Satan's instigation of Judas' treachery would cause particular anguish to a Master who loved this disciple but there is a certain justice in his engineering the circumstances of his own overthrow. In the mission of His Incarnation, Christ obliterated any influence Satan might have wielded through the introduction of sin into the world of men. When he drove out evil spirits and raised the dead to life, He demonstrated His supremacy over evil and the efficacy of his healing love.

It is splendidly appropriate that St John's record of Lazarus' being brought back from the dead *(11:1-45)* should be longer than the account of any other miracle because it pre-figures Christ's own Resurrection and our assurance of final victory. Any glee Satan might have had on Good Friday becomes his ultimate disappointment on Easter

Sunday. Hell's armies have fled though we, in our own moment of time, share in the conflict with an enemy whose hatred of God and those who adore Him remains unabated.

Reflection on the Fall

When Christ told the Pharisees and the Herodians to render to God and to Caesar their respective dues, He was reminding us that we belong to two worlds because we are citizens of earth and citizens of Heaven. In God's indivisible act of creation, our destiny is interwoven with that of the angels and we are not unaffected by the fall of some of them. It was their leader's envy that inspired his assault on God's chosen people in the person of Adam who was to follow his disobedient example.

Physical and moral evil

God is infinitely good and, therefore, the universe He created is good. In Jesus Christ we are redeemed once and for all and, in the light of eternity, there is no on-going struggle between God and Satan. We are renewed by the Holy Spirit and have the assurances of the saviour. When His seventy-two disciples came back rejoicing that the devils had submitted to them when they used His name, He told them that He the Word of God, had seen Satan "fall like lightning from Heaven." He then gave them power over the "whole strength of the enemy" and promised that nothing would ever hurt them. *(cf Lk 18:17-25)*.

Why do we still have problems?

If such is the case, why are we still beset by temptations, plagues, wars, inhumanity, physical and mental suffering and, ultimately, death? The stark reality is that, just like Satan and his followers, the human race lost an opportunity to show its love for its Creator and the created order was wounded by the original sin of disobedience which characterised all subsequent sins. At the root of sin is a decision to replace God with oneself by preferring one's inclinations to the worship to which he is entitled. If we do not worship Him, He allows us to go our own way and put up with the consequences we have chosen.

With the angels, mankind shared the dignity of freedom to choose in the context of all moral action and the choice we made left us with burdens to be shouldered. Fortunately, God does not remain aloof from our self-imposed plight and does not mean us to experience retribution. *(cf 1 Th 1:1-6; 9-11)*. His Providence is active and his plan is still realised through the freedom, not the coercion of His creatures for whose salvation He ceaselessly works.

Christ is lifted up and draws all things to Himself

We have God's merciful remedy so that all may be saved from sin and its consequences through faith in Jesus Christ who has paid every debt. The Son Of God adopts our wounded humanity and, through His Incarnation, suffering and death, takes on our burdens and renews our obedience through His incomparable suffering. He shows us how to resist Satan and, as the restores source of all grace, re-establishes our integral union with His Father. No one can understand better than He how temporarily difficult the human condition is, which is why He stays with us in the Sacrament of changeless love. Transcending time and space, His complete Sacrifice is presented to us with each celebration of the Eucharist. In union with His suffering, He invites us to stand at the foot of the Cross, not then but now. We can also run to the empty tomb and share the joy of His Resurrection from our fall. We have His Body to eat and His Blood to drink so that we can proclaim His death, and more easily accept ours, until He comes in glory. "I freed your shoulders from the burden; your hands were freed from the load; You called in distress and I saved you... O that my people would heed me... At once I would subdue their foes, turn my hand against their enemies."

Deliver us from evil

The Lord's Prayer discloses the range of God's economy of salvation. Our interdependence in the drama of sin and death becomes a solidarity in the Body of Christ, the Communion of Saints. When we pray for delivery from evil, we are asking God to display His Son's victory over Satan and this supplication we renew in the Communion Rite of the Eucharist. "Deliver us Lord from every evil and grant us peace in our day. In Your mercy keep us free from sin and protect us from all anxiety as we wait in joyful hope for the coming of our Saviour Jesus Christ."

"Rank on rank the host of Heaven
Spreads its vanguard on the way,
As the Light of light descendeth
from the realms of endless day,
that the powers of hell may vanish
as the darkness clears away.

"At His feet the six-winged Seraphs
Cherubim with sleepless eye,
veil their faces to the presence
as with ceaseless voice they cry,
alleluia, alleluia, alleluia, Lord most high."
(Liturgy of St James, tr. G. Moultrie, 1829-85).

Death

The most disconcerting result of mankind's fall is the end of our life on this earth. Death is, however, the entrance to our spiritual sphere and the restoration of integrity in God's presence which, from all eternity, He has intended for us. Christ, the Man, has pioneered the way through this gateway and waits to share with us His victory over death. Father, by Your power You bring us to birth and by Your Providence you rule our lives. We give You thanks through Jesus Christ Our

Lord by whose saving death the world, at Your command, is reborn and the dead rise again to life. We rise, at Your word to the glory of the Resurrection. *(Prefaces of Christian Burial, adapted)*.

THE FEASTS OF THE ARCHANGELS
SAINTS MICHAEL, GABRIEL, RAPHAEL

(September 29th)

Saint Michael

Michael *('Who is like unto God?')* makes an early appearance in the Old testament when he comes to the assistance of the prophet Daniel in a time of conflict. He is the leading prince of God's army and the protector of Israel. *(Dn 10:13)*. Reference has already been made to the Book of Revelation *(12:7-12)* which vividly describes how he, and the angels faithful to God, defeated Satan and his followers in a mighty battle and drove them out of heaven. The Christian church has always shown great devotion to St Michael. As the Kingdom of Heaven on earth it is appropriate that she acknowledge the part he played in foiling Satan's attempt to overthrow God's rule. After Mary, the Blessed Mother of God, he has place of honour in the Litany of the Saints, the 'Confiteor' and the Baptismal Liturgy.

History of the Devotion

The Emperor Constantine was so grateful for military victories he attributed to Michael's intervention that he built the Michaelion Basilica near Constantinople in his honour. This quickly became a place of pilgrimage for the Eastern Church and renowned for cures of the sick. It was soon joined by fifteen other churches which bore his name. There was such confidence in his intercession for the sick that, in Greece and Asia, even early health spas were called after him.

In the West, the Saint appeared in the fifth century to the Bishop of Siponto at monte Gargano in the Kingdom of Naples. The Church of St Michael, built on the site of the apparition became a centre of devout and efficacious pilgrimage and, until 1969, the event was celebrated by the whole Church with its own Feast on May 8th. Afterwards, churches consecrated to him multiplied, particularly in Rome. The most famous shrine in the West is Mont-St-Michel in Normandy, where a Benedictine monastery was founded in the tenth century to honour another apparition, celebrated locally on October 16th. After Germany's conversion, veneration replaced that previously accorded to the god Woden and numerous St Michael chapels became features of the mountain and forest districts.

The British Isles

Early devotion is exemplified by dedications at Malmesbury and a cemetery-oratory at Hexham is mentioned by St Bede. Skellig Michael in County Kerry and Saint Michael's Mount in Cornwall witness the

Archangel's eminence in the eyes of our ancestors and his association with geographical heights. In Mediaeval England, seven hundred churches carried his name and, here, much is owed to the Benedictines who came to the country after the Conquest. The Festival of Michaelmas was celebrated with great solemnity and, to-day, still identifies the autumn period of the academic and legal year.

Saint Gabriel

Gabriel *('Strength of God')* stands in God's presence and is His ambassador of revelation and intercession. He visited Daniel to teach him understanding and inform him that he was to rebuild Jerusalem in preparation for the coming of the Anointed Prince who would establish a New Covenant with man. *(Dn 9:20-27)*. He is the herald of salvation who announces the birth of John the Baptist, the last and greatest of the prophets who stands astride the two covenants. To him, God entrusts the announcement of the Incarnation to Mary, in whose motherhood God the Son becomes man, divine and human natures are united and the work of Redemption begun. *(Lk 1:11-20;26-32)*.

Gabriel and the life of Christ

When Joseph learned of Mary's pregnancy and decided to end their betrothal with delicacy, Gabriel is thought to have been that "angel of the Lord" who tells him, in a dream, not to be afraid to take her home as his wife

because she had conceived by the power of the Holy
Spirit. *(cf Mt 1:20)*. He gives the shepherds the news of
the Saviour's birth and selects them as the first visitors to
the Divine Child. They will confirm his earlier
annunciation so that Mary will treasure in her heart the
knowledge that her Son is the world's Redeemer. There is
a similarly pious but logical assumption that Gabriel
would have led the angelic choir in their acclamation,
"Glory to God in the highest heaven and peace to men of
good will." *(cf Lk 2:1-20)*. When the wise men from the
East have adored the new-born King and offered their
presents, we recognise Gabriel's solicitous co-ordination
in his advice to avoid Herod on their homeward journey.
St Joseph's sleep is not to be left undisturbed. Gabriel
urges him to get up and protect his family from Herod's
murderous intentions by escaping to Egypt. When Herod
is dead the angel, in another nocturnal visit, tells him to
return with them to Israel but, even as he travels, he has a
similar warning to go to Nazareth of Galilee rather than
Bethlehem of Judea. Antipas was ruler in Galilee but
Archelaus in Judea was even more of a threat. In
choosing the less dangerous, the angel and Joseph
enabled the fulfilment of the prophecy that Jesus Christ
would be called a Nazarene. *(cf. Mt 2)*.

The Fathers of the Church believed it was Gabriel, the
angel of the annunciation, who comforted Christ in His
Agony in the Garden. It is touchingly appropriate that the

same Archangel should watch over both the beginning and the end of His Lord's life on earth.

When we recite the first Joyful mystery of the Rosary and the Angelus, there is opportunity to revere the Blessed Virgin and her messenger and offer them a renewal of their joy at the moment of the Incarnation.

Saint Raphael

Raphael *('God heals')* introduces himself in the Book of Tobit as one of the seven angels always ready to stand in the glory of the Lord's presence. Tobit, suffering from blindness, was unable to help his son, Tobias, find someone to show him the way to Medina. Raphael, in human appearance, arrives and offers to be companion and guide on the journey. Tobias had been hoping to marry Sarah, the daughter of Raguel but the poor girl had been betrothed on seven previous occasions and each time, Asmodeus, "the worst of demons", had killed the intended but unfortunate bridegroom. When the young couple prayed to God for help, He sent Raphael who cured Tobit's blindness who, with God's light restored was able to bless the union of his son and Sarah and so rid her of Asmodeus' influence.

Raphael and the will of God

This Archangel offers further insight on the position of the angels in God's plan and their consequent relationship with us. He explains to Tobit and Tobias that, as the messenger of God, he hears the prayers of people on earth and presents them to Him. He is present, not by his own decision but because so wishes and it is he who must be praised and thanked through all ages. *(cf Tb 3: 7-17; 12:12-21).* The early Christians believed Raphael tended the wounds suffered by the martyrs and consoled them in their sufferings. He is invoked as a comforter of the sick to whom he may bring renewed health if that is what God wishes. The Fathers were of the opinion that it was of Raphael whom St John had in mind when he described the sheep-pool in Jerusalem and the Bethzatha building's five porches where the afflicted waited for the pool's water to move. "At intervals, the angel of the Lord came down and the water was disturbed and the first person to enter the water after this disturbance was cured." *(Jn 5:1-4).* In 1921, Pope Benedict XV declared St Raphael the Patron of post-office, telephone and telegraph workers.

From the Liturgy

"Bless the Lord, all you His angels; mighty in power, you obey His word and heed the sound of his voice." *(Entrance Antiphon)*

"God our Father, you guide the work of angels and of men: may those who serve You constantly in Heaven keep our lives safe from all harm here on earth." *(Opening Prayer)*

"The Lord's sovereignty is an eternal sovereignty which shall never pass away, nor will His empire ever be destroyed." *(Dn 7:13-14)*

"Jesus said, 'I tell you most solemnly, you will see heaven laid open and, above the Son of Man, the angels of God ascending and descending.'"*(Jn 1:50-51)*

"Father, all powerful and ever-living God, we do well, always and everywhere, to give you thanks. In praising Your faithful angels, we also praise Your glory for in honouring them we honour You, their Creator. Their splendour shows us Your greatness which surpasses in goodness the whole of creation. Through Christ our Lord the great army of angels rejoices in Your glory. In adoration and joy, we make their hymn of praise our own: Holy, Holy, Holy Lord, God of power and might; heaven and earth are full of Your glory." *(Preface of the Angels)*

"Father, as You laid the foundations of creation, the stars of the morning sang for joy and the sons of God, in chorus, chanted Your praise. They stand before Your throne to proclaim you and you send them to us for our well-being and protection. At your coming they sang of peace towards men. May their message inspire the hearts of rulers and peoples. We too are called to be angels of light. Keep us pure in mind and body and may Your church never fail in Your praise."*(Liturgy of the Hours, Intercessions, adapted)*

"Whenever a mighty deed is in question, Michael is assigned, so that by his actions and name it may be made known that no one can do what God can do. So, in the case of our ancient enemy who, in his pride, wanted to be like God when he said: 'I will ascend to heaven; above the stars of God I will set my throne on high; I will make myself like the Most High': when he is shown to be condemned to eternal punishment at the end of the world, he is described as about to do battle with Michael. As the author of Revelation says, 'War broke out with Michael the Archangel.'

Gabriel was sent to Mary, for Gabriel means 'Strength of God'. He came to announce Him who deigned to be lowly so as to wage war on the spiritual powers of the air. He who came as God of power and as one strong in battle, was to be announced by Gabriel, the 'Strength of God'.

Raphael is the healing of God since he wiped away the shadows of blindness from Tobit when he touched his eyes to cure him. The one who is sent to cure was, indeed, worthy of the name 'Healing of God'."

(From the Homilies of Pope St Gregory the Great, 540-604, Office of Readings of the Feast).

Prayer to St Michael

"Holy Michael the Archangel,
Defend us in the day of battle.
Be our protection against the wickedness and snares of

the devil; May God rebuke him, we humbly pray;
And do thou, Prince of the heavenly host,
By the power of God,
thrust into hell Satan and all evil spirits who wander
through the world For the ruin of souls. Amen."

(The Prayer of Pope Leo XIII, once said by the Celebrant after every Mass, other than a High Mass. In the light of the Church's recent reminders of the teaching about indulgences, it may be useful to mention that a three-year indulgence is attached to the recitation and, under the usual conditions, a plenary indulgence once a month if the prayer has been said daily).

THE FEAST OF THE HOLY GUARDIAN ANGELS

(October 2nd)

The Old Testament

In the Book of Exodus, God speaks to Moses and establishes His Covenant with the Israelites. He promises to send an angel to guard them and conduct them to the Promised Land of Canaan which is a part of that which is known as Palestine. He exhorts His people to give reverence to His angel and attend carefully to his words. *(Ex 23:20-23)*. Such an Angel of the Covenant represents God's own Son, His messenger and our Redeemer, in anticipation of the Incarnation. Christ goes before His followers to prepare a place for them and appoints an angel to watch over them as they journey to the promised land of God's Kingdom.

In Psalm 90, which was most likely written by King David, there is an assurance of protection for mankind who will be delivered from the malice of the powers of darkness by the King of Kings.

"No disaster can overtake you, no plague will come near your dwelling; He will put you in His angels' charge to guard you wherever you go. They will support you on their hands in case you hurt your foot against a stone." *(10-13)*

When David was being pursued by his enemy, Saul, he had to take refuge in a cave and was feeling very sorry for himself. "The enemy pursues my soul; he has crushed my life to the ground," but he has confidence in God whom he begs to rescue him and send "His good spirit" to guide him to a smooth path. *(Ps 143)*. Our Lord Himself prayed the Psalms and we, too, can make them our own especially when in need of guidance and protection.

The New Testament

We are all God's children, so when Christ stressed the importance of child-like qualities because the children's angels are in the presence of His Father, He was excluding no one. *(Mt 13:41-42)*. God's angels belong to trusting 'little ones' and display the tender love for all His 'children' who, with them, are made to be with Him and see the vision of His Beauty.

The Teaching of the Catholic Church

"From infancy to death, human life is surrounded by the watchful care and intercession of the Guardian Angels. Beside each one stands an angel as protector and shepherd leading him to life. Already, here on earth, the Christian life shares, by faith, in the blessed company of angels and mankind united in God." *(Catechism of the Catholic Church, 336)*

Other reflections

Origen, 185-254 AD, whose philosophy contributed to the early Church's schools of thought, said that "the presence of the angels who watch over us and minister to God, is with anyone who prays, so that the angels are united with him in what he asks in prayer." St Augustine, 354-430, taught that "these blessed spirits have the tenderest affection for the faithful in their care; they see in them, fellow citizens destined to fill in heaven the places which the revolt of the angels left vacant. St John Baptist de La Salle, 1651-1719, asks us "to show special love for those whom God has appointed to guard us from the first moment of our life. Our guardian Angels watch over us in all places and act as mediators between our selves and God. They help our labours, protect us while we sleep, encourage us in our trials and rejoice in our victory. Ask their assistance, thank them for their goodness and avoid everything that would cause them sorrow."

"Angel of the Lord, my faithful guardian to whom the Divine Goodness has entrusted me, enlighten, protect, direct and govern me always. Amen.

From the Liturgy

"God our Father, in Your loving providence you send your holy angels to watch over us. Hear our prayers, defend us always by their protection and let us share your life with them forever." *(Opening Prayer)*

"In those days, I heard in my vision the voices of a multitude of angels standing on every side of the throne where the living figures of the elders were, in thousands of thousands, crying aloud, 'Power and Godhead, wisdom and strength, honour and glory and blessing are His by right, the Lamb that was slain." *(Rv 5:11-12)*

"They are present, and present to you, not merely accompanying you. They are present in order to protect you. Though it is He who gave them this charge, we should not be ungrateful to them, for they obey with such love and help us in great need. Let us love His angels...they will be our co-heirs in the future while now they are our guardians. What have we to fear with such protectors who cannot be vanquished, be led astray or lead us astray?... They are faithful, wise, powerful. Let us follow and cling to them and we shall abide in the presence of the Almighty." *(Sermon 12 of St Bernard, 1090-1153, The Office of Readings)*

"Lord, we pray that you will visit this dwelling of ours and drive far from it all the snares of the enemy. Let your holy angels stay with us to keep us in peace and may Your blessing be ever upon us." *(Prayer of Compline, Liturgy of the Hours)*

"Give praise to the Lord in Heaven; praise Him, all that dwell on high. Praise Him all you angels of His; praise Him all His armies." *(Ps 148, Votive Mass of the Angels)*

"Angels for my witnesses, I sing of Thy praises. I bow down in worship towards Thy sanctuary, giving thanks to Thy name." *(Ps 137, Votive Mass of the Angels)*

Hymnology

Sometimes the concentrated beauty and meaning of inspired poetry can be veiled by attention to a melody or the diversity of voices raised in prayerful song. Two examples are offered for private thought.

"Great God...doth not Thy Providence
Send earth-frequenting angels to succour us,
Their charge to keep Thy wayward children
Holy of heart in the midst of evil?

Else might the unseen author of wickedness
Waylay our footsteps, heedlessly wandering,
Nor spare the souls Christ died to ransom,
Scattered like sheep for the wolf to tear them."
(Regnator orbis summus et arbiter, J.B. de Santeuil, 1630-97)

"They come God's messengers of love,
They come from realms of peace above,
From homes of never fading light,
From blissful mansions ever bright.

They come to watch around us here,
To soothe our sorrow, calm our fear:
O heavenly guides, speed not away,
God willeth you with us to stay."
*(Hymn for the Liturgy of the Hours, October 2nd,
R. Campbell, 1814-68)*

ANGELS IN THE NEW AGE

"O God, You are my God, for You I long; for You my soul is thirsting. My body pines for you like a dry, weary land without water. So I gaze on You in the sanctuary to see Your strength and Your glory. For Your love is better than life... My soul clings to You; Your right hand holds me fast." *(Ps 62). 6 3*

The prayer of King David in the wilderness of Judah reveals the human soul conscious of a spiritual destiny. The body lives in a material world where fulfilment seems dependent on wealth, status, relationships, gratification, enlarged experience and change. The soul experiences an unease, a feeling of incompleteness, like a symphony left unfinished. Through God's mercy, there is occasional joy, pleasure, light-heartedness but, by the nature of this world, total happiness and security cannot be grasped. St Augustine found the answer to his unease in striving for an intimate relationship with God but, because this is Heaven, it cannot be fully realised in this life. Sometimes, in our dreams, God gives us a sense of absolute peace, an absence of all anxiety and frustration. It disappears as we awake but we are grateful for an intimation of a blessed immortality. St Paul encourages us to use an imagination which is guided by the Holy Spirit and explore the nature of our spiritual being and destiny. Despite the inadequacy of description of what is outside experience, he urges us to open our minds to the fullness of an inexpressible truth. "We groan inwardly as we wait for our bodies to be set free (but) what we suffer in this life can never be compared to the glory, as yet unrevealed, which is waiting for us." *(Rm 8:18-25)*. In our own day, the Church responds to St Paul's invitation and celebrates membership of the angels' spiritual world in a Morning Prayer hymn *(e.g. Saturday, Week One)*.

"It were my soul's desire to see the face of God;
It were my soul's desire to rest in His abode.
Grant, Lord, my soul's desire, deep waves of
cleansing sighs, Grant, Lord, my soul's desire
from earthly cares to rise.

It were my soul's desire to imitate my King,
It were my soul's desire His endless praise to sing.
It were my soul's desire when Heaven's gate is won
To find my soul's desire clear shining like the sun.
This, still my soul's desire, whatever life afford,
To gain my soul's desire and see Thy face, O Lord."

Inspired human initiative has enlivened the truth of the spiritual, even to the extent of identifying our angelic companions into categories and honouring them in the celebration of their Feasts. Their fellowship and our co-operation in doing God's will is precisely what His Revelation intended. However, in a search for the other-worldly, it is prudent to remember that questions will not always be answered by science, religious faith or the unaided, human intellect and that one of Christ's first instructions to His disciples was to cast out unclean spirits. Satan can still present himself as the angel who carries light and his troops can adopt the most convincing poses.

The Church is sensitive to the aspirations of other faiths and reminds us that Christ desires all to be saved. "There are those who, though innocently ignorant of Christ's Gospel and His Church, search for God in sincerity of heart and attempt to carry out His will through the dictate of conscience." It advises, however, that "if men are deceived by the devil, thinking becomes futile, the truth about God exchanged for a lie and the creature served in preference to the Creator." *(Dogmatic Constitution on the Church, 16).*

New Age enlightenment

A cursory look at what is loosely described as New Ageism, may be of some use when distinguishing between genuine and false angels. Not all New Age followers necessarily share the same creed or subscribe to the details of belief with universal conviction or intensity, but the mention of some characteristics will not be unjust. Generally speaking, it would appear that salvation is considered attainable by knowing and experiencing one's own 'divine' nature. In a pantheistic universe, 'god' is everything and everything is 'god', so man must be 'divine' and, as a component of the 'godhead' or 'cosmic force', creates 'god' in his own image. Man is 'god' because God is not a person but merely the expression of 'transpersonal awareness' and 'cosmic energy'. This is reminiscent of something heard before, perhaps in the Garden of Eden.

In a New Age, fulfilment can be achieved through a process of cleansing during a series of re-incarnations in which the consequences of a predecessors actions are bequeathed to a successor. As his own authority, man is free to choose what are regarded as rights but which are not, necessarily, related to responsibilities. Suffering is of no value and death may be regarded as a euphoric experience giving access to another life-cycle. The rainbow, an adopted symbol of spiritual and economic influence, is a bridge by which man crosses to a universe of 'ordered reality'. Truth is based upon personal 'divinity' and measured by the harmonious results of ecstasy, 'oceanic feeling' and relaxation.

Christ is dismissed as a mere mortal who, through 'enlightenment', reached a superhuman eminence like Buddha or Krishna. He and His Christianity do not offer the only way to God and He is only an example of the 'divinity' each one achieves by enlightenment. This internal enlightenment, with self-absorbed introspection and the vague expectation of universal harmony, replaces faith, prayer and the Gospel message. Such a theory contrasts sharply with Christian teaching that Utopia is not for this world and this mortal life is but a prelude to the Beatific Vision of God.

Some New Age doctrines are ecology based, rather like Creation Spirituality and a cult of personality finds no need for a ministerial priesthood or sacramental structures. Corollaries include the myth of 'Gaia', a goddess religion of Mother-Earth, witchcraft, spiritualism, psychic and paranormal phenomena and the veneration of Lucifer as a hero of enlightenment and individualism. Self-styled gurus and 'divinities', like the '7th Angel of Revelation',who claim to have received telepathic communications from celestial powers have, sadly, led their followers to disaster.

New Age and Christianity.

There is some antipathy towards the masculine concepts, images and metaphors of God and institutional worship. An exchange between and among various beliefs is preferred. Feminist theology finds the patriarchal doctrine of the Trinity unacceptable while religion centred upon Christ the Man can be regarded by some as a source of conflict and discomfort. For others, a golden age has either dawned, or is expected soon, when the Vernal Equinox passes from Pisces, with it Christianity connotations to the water-carrier

Aquarius, presumably identified as an alternative and more acceptable source of life-giving water than Christ. *(cf Jn 4:5-42)*. Christ's reign will succumb to the age of Aquarius when people managing cosmic forces, and summoning the inhabitants of the spiritual sphere at will, will attain peace, harmony, love and sexual liberation.

Christ's Church

We have the wisdom and experience of the Church, guided by the Holy Spirit, to guide our search for genuine spirituality and mysticism removed from myth and superstition. She counsels against those distortions of collective imagination and individual curiosity which can harm body and soul. Contrary to some New Age belief, God's angels who accompany our spiritual journey are neither masculine nor feminine, nor flying super-humans who can be called in from the cosmos. They are not related to, UFO crews or the spirits of ancient folk-lore who roam the environment, often as combatants in an imagined war between the sun and the moon, a struggle between light and darkness. They are not the 'angelic' "Ascendant Masters" of the 'Breatharian' philosophy which holds that the human frame can survive on 'light' for its sustenance.

Angels are dependent

Since they are created by God, dependent on Him and rejoice to do His will, they are not alternative deities or self-employed conjuring tricksters. The angel who touched a rock with his staff to produce the fire which consumed Gideon's meat and cakes, for example, was demonstrating God's reassuring power so that a fearful general would find the confidence to lead the Israelite army against the hostile Medianites. *(Jg 6:11-24)*. In the 'Acts of the Apostles', we read that Simon the Magician misled people with his assumed 'divine' powers until Philip's preaching converted him and, in Cyprus, the baleful influence of Elymas Magos had to be removed by the purposeful intervention of Paul and Barnabas. *(cf Ac 8,13)*

For our guidance

In our day, the Church teaches that forms of divination which call upon Satan and his demons, attempts to involve the dead in disclosure of the future, spiritism, witchcraft and having recourse to the occult are contrary to the adoration which we owe only to God and which is the first subject of His Commandments. *(cf 'Catechism of the Catholic Church', 2115-7)*

Informative Catholic Reading

We hope that you have enjoyed reading this booklet.

If you would like to find out more about CTS booklets - we'll send you our free information pack and catalogue.

Please send us your details:

Name ....

Address ....

....

....

Postcode ....

Telephone..

Email ....

Send to: CTS, 40-46 Harleyford Road,
                Vauxhall, London
                SE11 5AY

Tel: 020 7640 0042
Fax: 020 7640 0046
Email: info@cts-online.org.uk